In Celebration Of

_____

_____

Date

_____

Guests

Name

Best Wishes and Messages

Guests

Name

Best Wishes and Messages

Guests

Name

Best Wishes and Messages

Guests

Name

Best Wishes and Messages

_____

_____

_____

_____

_____

_____

_____

_____

_____

_____

_____

_____

_____

Guests

Name

Best Wishes and Messages

Guests

Name

Best Wishes and Messages

Guests

Name

Best Wishes and Messages

Guests

Name

Best Wishes and Messages

Guests

Name

Best Wishes and Messages

_____

_____

_____

_____

_____

_____

_____

_____

_____

_____

_____

_____

Guests

Name

Best Wishes and Messages

Guests

Name

Best Wishes and Messages

Guests

Name

Best Wishes and Messages

_____

_____

_____

_____

_____

_____

_____

_____

_____

_____

_____

_____

_____

Guests

Name

Best Wishes and Messages

_____

_____

_____

_____

_____

_____

_____

_____

_____

_____

_____

_____

Guests

Name

Best Wishes and Messages

_____

_____

_____

_____

_____

_____

_____

_____

_____

_____

_____

_____

_____

Guests

Name

Best Wishes and Messages

Guests

Name

Best Wishes and Messages

_____

_____

_____

_____

_____

_____

_____

_____

_____

_____

_____

_____

Guests

Name

Best Wishes and Messages

Guests

Name

Best Wishes and Messages

Guests

Name

Best Wishes and Messages

Guests

Name

Best Wishes and Messages

Guests

Name

Best Wishes and Messages

Guests

Name

Best Wishes and Messages

_____

_____

_____

_____

_____

_____

_____

_____

_____

_____

_____

_____

_____

Guests

Name

Best Wishes and Messages

Guests

Name

Best Wishes and Messages

Guests

Name

Best Wishes and Messages

Guests

Name

Best Wishes and Messages

Guests

Name

Best Wishes and Messages

_____

_____

_____

_____

_____

_____

_____

_____

_____

_____

_____

Guests

Name

Best Wishes and Messages

_____

_____

_____

Guests

Name

Best Wishes and Messages

_____

_____

_____

_____

_____

_____

_____

_____

_____

_____

_____

_____

Guests

Name

Best Wishes and Messages

Guests

Name

Best Wishes and Messages

_____

_____

_____

_____

_____

_____

_____

_____

_____

_____

_____

_____

Guests

Name

Best Wishes and Messages

_____

_____

_____

_____

_____

_____

_____

_____

_____

_____

_____

_____

Guests

Name

Best Wishes and Messages

Guests

Name

Best Wishes and Messages

_____

_____

_____

_____

_____

_____

_____

_____

_____

_____

_____

_____

_____

Guests

Name

Best Wishes and Messages

_____

_____

_____

_____

_____

_____

_____

_____

_____

_____

_____

_____

Guests

Name

Best Wishes and Messages

_____

_____

_____

_____

_____

_____

_____

_____

_____

_____

_____

_____

_____

Guests

Name

Best Wishes and Messages

Guests

Name

Best Wishes and Messages

_____

_____

_____

_____

_____

_____

_____

_____

_____

_____

_____

Guests

Name

Best Wishes and Messages

Guests

Name

Best Wishes and Messages

_____

_____

_____

_____

_____

_____

_____

_____

_____

_____

_____

Guests

Name

Best Wishes and Messages

_____

_____

_____

_____

_____

_____

_____

_____

_____

_____

_____

_____

Guests

Name

Best Wishes and Messages

_____

_____

_____

_____

_____

_____

_____

_____

_____

_____

_____

Guests

Name

Best Wishes and Messages

Guests

Name

Best Wishes and Messages

_____

_____

_____

_____

_____

_____

_____

_____

_____

_____

_____

_____

_____

Guests

Name

Best Wishes and Messages

Guests

Name

Best Wishes and Messages

Guests

Name

Best Wishes and Messages

_____

_____

_____

_____

_____

_____

_____

_____

_____

_____

_____

_____

Guests

Name

Best Wishes and Messages

_____

_____

_____

_____

_____

_____

_____

_____

_____

_____

_____

_____

_____

Guests

Name

Best Wishes and Messages

Guests

Name

Best Wishes and Messages

Guests

Name

Best Wishes and Messages

Guests

Name

Best Wishes and Messages

Guests

Name

Best Wishes and Messages

Guests

Name

Best Wishes and Messages

Guests

Name

Best Wishes and Messages

Guests

Name

Best Wishes and Messages

_____

_____

_____

_____

_____

_____

_____

_____

_____

_____

_____

_____

Guests

Name

Best Wishes and Messages

Guests

Name

Best Wishes and Messages

_____

_____

_____

_____

_____

_____

_____

_____

_____

_____

_____

_____

_____

Guests

Name

Best Wishes and Messages

Guests

Name

Best Wishes and Messages

Guests

Name

Best Wishes and Messages

Guests

Name

Best Wishes and Messages

_____

_____

_____

Guests

Name

Best Wishes and Messages

_____

_____

_____

_____

_____

_____

_____

_____

_____

_____

_____

Guests

Name

Best Wishes and Messages

_____

_____

_____

_____

_____

_____

_____

_____

_____

_____

_____

_____

Guests

Name

Best Wishes and Messages

_____

_____

_____

_____

_____

_____

_____

_____

_____

_____

_____

_____

Guests

Name

Best Wishes and Messages

_____

_____

_____

_____

_____

_____

_____

_____

_____

_____

_____

Guests

Name

Best Wishes and Messages

Guests

Name

Best Wishes and Messages

_____

_____

_____

_____

_____

_____

_____

_____

_____

_____

_____

_____

Guests

Name

Best Wishes and Messages

_____

_____

_____

_____

_____

_____

_____

_____

_____

_____

Guests

Name

Best Wishes and Messages

_____

_____

_____

_____

_____

_____

_____

_____

_____

_____

_____

_____

Guests

Name

Best Wishes and Messages

_____

_____

_____

_____

_____

_____

_____

_____

_____

_____

_____

Guests

Name

Best Wishes and Messages

Guests

Name

Best Wishes and Messages

_____

_____

_____

_____

_____

_____

_____

_____

_____

_____

_____

_____

Guests

Name

Best Wishes and Messages

_____

_____

_____

_____

_____

_____

_____

_____

_____

_____

_____

_____

_____

_____

Guests

Name

Best Wishes and Messages

_____

_____

_____

_____

_____

_____

_____

_____

_____

_____

_____

Guests

Name

Best Wishes and Messages

Guests

Name

Best Wishes and Messages

Guests

Name

Best Wishes and Messages

Guests

Name

Best Wishes and Messages

Guests

Name

Best Wishes and Messages

_____

_____

_____

_____

_____

_____

_____

_____

_____

_____

_____

_____

_____

_____

Photo

Gift Log

Gift Log

GIFT RECEIVED	GIVEN BY	THANK YOU

Gift Log

GIFT RECEIVED	GIVEN BY	THANK YOU

Gift Log

GIFT RECEIVED	GIVEN BY	THANK YOU

Gift Log

GIFT RECEIVED	GIVEN BY	THANK YOU

Gift Log

GIFT RECEIVED	GIVEN BY	THANK YOU

Gift Log

GIFT RECEIVED	GIVEN BY	THANK YOU

Gift Log

GIFT RECEIVED	GIVEN BY	THANK YOU

Gift Log

GIFT RECEIVED	GIVEN BY	THANK YOU

Gift Log

GIFT RECEIVED	GIVEN BY	THANK YOU

Gift Log

GIFT RECEIVED	GIVEN BY	THANK YOU

Gift Log

GIFT RECEIVED	GIVEN BY	THANK YOU

Gift Log

GIFT RECEIVED	GIVEN BY	THANK YOU

Made in the USA
Monee, IL
15 December 2021

85280332R00059